chartered
management
institute

inspiring leaders

The leading organisation for professional management

As the champion of management, the Chartered Management Institute shapes and supports the managers of tomorrow. By sharing intelligent insights and setting standards in management development, the Institute helps to deliver results in a dynamic world.

Setting and raising standards

The Institute is a nationally accredited organisation, responsible for setting standards in management and recognising excellence through the award of professional qualifications.

Encouraging development, improving performance

The Institute has a vast range of development programmes, qualifications, information resources and career guidance to help managers and their organisations meet new challenges in a fast-changing environment.

Shaping opinion

With in-depth research and regular policy surveys of its 91,000 individual members and 520 corporate members, the Chartered Management Institute has a deep understanding of the key issues. Its view is informed, intelligent and respected.

For more information call 01536 204222 or visit www.managers.org.uk

C O N T E N T S

Have you ever wondered why some people seem to succeed almost effortlessly whenever they go for an interview? Perhaps they are just 'lucky'. We think not! Their performance, and ultimately their success, is the result of thorough personal preparation.

You too can improve your ability and success through a combination of thought, training, practice and experience. *Succeeding at Interviews in a Week* is your companion in this process. By setting time aside for each day, you will be guided on your route to success.

Sunday	The interview process
Monday	Do your research
Tuesday	Know yourself
Wednesday	Preparing yourself for success
Thursday	Responding skilfully
Friday	Your moves
Saturday	Putting it all together

You are now making the first significant investment in improving your interview performance – congratulations! Now read on . . .

The interview process

You opened the post this morning to find you have been
invited to an interview – great news! You feel good. You are
high, elated and you congratulate yourself. You imagine
yourself in the role; it's exciting, an ideal job for you. You
read the letter again and, as the reality of the interview
becomes your focus, you are bombarded with less positive
feelings and thoughts, such as:

- I hate interviews
- I can't remember the last time I was interviewed
- I really want this job – I hope I don't let myself down

It is not uncommon to feel a degree of trepidation in
anticipation of an interview. The trick is not to let this weigh
you down.

After all, you have experienced being interviewed, not just
once but many times in your career. Most career transitions
such as selection, promotion or other forms of career
development will have been punctuated by interviews. You
are therefore experienced and familiar with the process. As
interviews follow a relatively common format, you will
already have some of the skills and knowledge required to
make you successful.

This experience is not always reflected in your performance.
The following comments from interviewers reflect common
problems:

- She looked great on paper
- I know a lot about his employer, but very little about him
- She seemed very nervous and aggressive
- He stumbled over all the questions related to his personality
- I'm not sure how long he would stay
- She seemed too good to be true
- There was no substance in what he said
- It was difficult to get a word in edgeways

Think back over past interviews and answer the following question honestly: *Did I present myself in the best possible light?*

Whilst we would hope that your answer is 'yes', it is more likely to be 'no' or 'not quite'. Managers are often experienced interviewers, having undergone training on skills, techniques and questioning. They are not so skilled at being interviewed.

Having had experiences of being interviewed and being the interviewer, you will be aware that interviews often follow a tried and tested pattern. Today, we will help you focus on the known rather than the unpredictable factors, exploring questions such as why, in what way and by whom:

> *The interview process*
> * Interview objectives
> * Types of questions
> * Interviewers

Interview objectives

If you have been invited to an interview – well done! Your invitation is based on the limited knowledge the interviewer has of you from an application, recommendation or your past achievements. They already believe that you could be the person they are looking for. The interview is therefore an opportunity for interviewers to extend their knowledge and complete their picture of you.

You will have your own agenda. The interview is an opportunity for you to discover further information about the job and the organisation. Based on that information you can reach decisions about match and suitability.

The interview is a two-way process: treat it as such.

Interviewee's objectives are to:
- Gain the initiative – an offer or commitment
- Present yourself in the best possible light
- Make known your talents and expertise
- Fill gaps in knowledge about the job and organisation
- Meet future colleagues/managers
- Be clear about whether or not to accept the post

Interviewer's objectives are to:
- Find the most suitable person
- Encourage you to express yourself fully
- Look for specific skills and achievements
- Sell the job and organisation
- Assess your initial impact and social fit
- Appoint the right person

You will both have independent objectives with a degree of overlap. Spend time before the interview clarifying your objectives. You may even want to rank them; having gone through this process, you can be much clearer about whether the interview matches your objectives and, if not, for what reason.

Interview structure
The whole of the recruitment process requires careful planning. From drawing up a job description and person specification, designing the advertisement, compiling the information pack, to short-listing. The interview is no exception.

Be aware that interviewers will have clarified their objectives in general and decided on a format and a set of questions for each interviewee. No two interviews are the same. Your personality, application, cv, and experience will be different from others, as will the areas that require further exploration because they are of particular interest or concern. Whilst interviews are not the same, there are similarities, and there is a process which is common and accepted.

The process can be likened to a sandwich. It is built on some 'warm up' questions to help you both settle down and feel as comfortable as you can. The middle and main section of the interview will constitute the filling in the sandwich, where you will be asked a variety of questions, checking and clarifying match and suitability.

In the final stage there will be time for your questions, closing with a summary of the interview and an indication of what will happen next: a second interview, a meeting with other staff members, or a letter telling you the result of the interview.

Some organisations provide their interviewers with a standard form to assess certain aspects of the interviewee and their performance. They will have a points allocation for each category and make direct comparisons between candidates. Depending on the post available, they may cover the following:

Assessment categories
- Skills
- Knowledge
- Behaviour
- Motivation
- Fit with team
- Fit with culture
- Career aspirations

Types of questions

During your interview you will encounter a number of different types of questions. If you can recognise these and the reasons they are being asked, you can concentrate on your replies. We will give you further guidance on responding to questions on Thursday.

The better the questions, the better the interview. Questions can be categorised in the following ways:

- Open
- Probing
- Closed
- Hypothetical
- Leading
- Difficult
- Negative
- Discriminatory

Open questions
This is where interviewers give you the chance to talk. They want to hear your ideas and see how you develop an answer. Open questions usually start with:

- Who, What, Where, When, Which, Why and How

For example:
- What levels of budget responsibility have you had throughout your career?
- How did you implement Investors in People?

Questions such as these allow you the opportunity to sell yourself. They require a level of preparation on your part. Think about the key themes that are likely to be covered in the interview focusing on those which you consider will be of interest to the interviewer.

Probing
When interviewers are particularly interested in your reply and want further information, they will use probing questions to focus in on the subject:

For example:
- Tell me about your research to date
- How did you manage the change?
- What made you respond in that way?

It's rather like a funnelling process where the interviewer moves from general questions to specific examples.

Closed questions
Direct questions that tend to pin you down to a factual reply
or to a 'yes' or 'no' answer.

For example:
  • Were you responsible for managing a budget in your
    last job?
  • Are you familiar with Investors in People?

Questions such as these can inhibit you and restrict your
freedom in presenting information. For example, you may
not have been responsible for the budget in your last post,
but have had budget responsibilities in the past. If you are
not able to communicate this information it may reduce
your chances of being successful. Always try to highlight
relevant previous experience.

Hypothetical questions
Hypothetical questions are just that, encouraging you to
imagine how you might handle the unknown. They also

provide an opportunity for you to demonstrate how well you think and the quality of your judgement. The interviewer will suggest a hypothetical situation and ask how you would deal with it.

> *For example:*
> • What would you do if . . .?
> • How would you deal with . . .?
> • What would you expect from a perfect manager?

These can tend to be difficult questions to answer, especially if complex scenarios are being presented. If you are not careful you can end up tying yourself in knots, especially if you concentrate too much on trying to work out what kind of answer you think they might want. Try to relate these questions to your own experience and, if you are not clear about the complete details of the situation, ask for more information.

Leading questions
These are the opposite to hypothetical questions as here, the interviewer steers you to the kind of answer they expect. Leading questions do not give interviewers much of an idea about you, though you will have an insight into their thinking. Generally it is best not to rock the boat; go where the questions are leading and check if you are unclear.

> *For example:*
> • As you have had experience of budgeting, I'm sure you wouldn't . . .
> • With regard to Investors in People, you are obviously aware of the problems with . . .

Difficult questions

These take many shapes and forms. Give yourself a moment to think, rather than trying to start answering immediately. Don't be evasive; you may have some ideas about which areas of questioning are likely to cause you difficulty. Anticipate what areas interviewers might cover and be ready for them. It is important to have some kind of answer ready rather than clamming up and leaving interviewers to jump to their own, possibly incorrect, conclusions.

For example:
- I see you have a gap of 3 years in your employment; what did you do during that time?
- This job requires a professional diploma. How are you going to make up the shortfall in your qualifications?

You don't know which questions will take you by surprise. Whatever they are, take your time over them. And remember that in most cases, the interviewer is trying to give you the opportunity to put yourself forward in the best possible light, not trying to trip you up.

Negative questions

These can often reflect an interviewer's tendency to look on the more negative side of life. It may be their way of making comparisons between the best candidates.

For example:
- What are your weaknesses?
- Why is it that you have changed jobs so often?
- You stayed in your last job for 10 years. Why so long?

Don't fall into the trap of defending yourself, as though this were a direct attack by the interviewer. Be constructive and turn the question around to show yourself in a positive light.

Discriminatory questions

These sorts of questions are still asked at interview, particularly of women and minority groups.

Women applying for senior jobs may be confronted with a whole battery of questions about their private lives, which male colleagues might not be asked.

For example:
- How does your husband feel about you applying for this post?
- What effect might the increased responsibility have on your family life?
- Are you planning to have a family?

People from minority groups may be asked:

For example:
- How would you respond to criticism from a white colleague?

These all need to be handled very carefully. You need to clarify the interviewer's intention and the relevance of the question. Ask yourself and maybe even the interviewer:

- Is this question ever put to other candidates?
- Would it affect my performance in the role?

It could be that the interviewer is just clumsy rather than malicious.

If you feel that you have been discriminated against in your interview, you can contact the Equal Opportunities Commission who will advise you about what action to take.

Equal Opportunities Commission
Overseas House
Quay Street
Manchester M3 3HN
Tel: 0161 833 9244
Fax: 0161 835 1657
www.eoc.org.uk

As well as recognising the different types of questions, it is worth considering the order in which the questions are asked. The use of supplementary and probing questions will often suggest what is in the interviewer's mind; you should notice this and react accordingly.

Good interviewers will be watching your reactions and body language: posture, gestures and facial expressions. You should do the same; some interviewers deliberately present an unresponsive, wooden mask. This can be because they are inexperienced or are not comfortable with the role. With practice you should be able to read and assess intentions and reactions reasonably well. You will undoubtedly also meet some ineffective interviewers.

Interviewers

Interviewers are trained, not born! Be prepared for an interviewer who:

- Has not read your cv
- Gets aggressive to see how you react under stress
- Is constantly disturbed
- Makes remarks about your previous employer or boss
- Asks questions but doesn't listen to your answers

Even the best training can fall on deaf ears and even the best interviewers can have a bad day. If you happen to be on the receiving end of poor interviewing, you can sometimes turn it to your advantage. You may meet interviewers who fall into the following categories.

The disorganised interviewer
Allow them time to settle down and find the papers or notes that they need. Establish your preparedness early on and, if necessary, subtly suggest an interview structure.

The unprepared interviewer

Sometimes very experienced interviewers think they can sail
in on the day and don't need to prepare. You have to keep
calm and be patient. It won't do your cause any good if you
try to catch them out or show them up. If interviewers have
a position of authority over the post, you may want to
consider how you would feel working with them.

The nervous interviewer

You sense that the interviewer would rather be anywhere else
than in an interview room and may even be more nervous
than you are. This sometimes happens when specialist
functional managers are taken out of their familiar work
setting and are expected to be at ease in a more social setting.
They will be grateful if you offer relevant information and
loosely control the interview. Be careful not to patronise.

The aggressive interviewer

Don't allow aggressive interviewers to provoke you. Rather
than apologising for the weaknesses, failings or gaps in your
cv that they point out to you, give positive explanations and
put over what you have prepared.

Being familiar with the process of the interview will enable
you to understand the direction it is taking. If you are
unclear about a question, try to assess what the reasons are
for asking it and answer it accordingly.

Summary

We have begun the week with a general overview on the
process of interviews, preparing you generally for what you
should expect.

The interview process
- Objectives of an interview
  - interviewers' objectives
  - your objectives

- Types of question to expect
  - open
  - closed
  - hypothetical
  - difficult
  - negative
- Types and styles of interviewer
  - disorganised
  - unprepared
  - nervous
  - aggressive

Remember that interviews are not a new experience for you. Learn from the past to prepare you for the future.

Do your research

It is a natural human reaction to feel nervous and apprehensive going into a situation where you feel uncertain. As we suggested yesterday, interviews have common features. There are however aspects which are unique and unpredictable. No two experiences of being interviewed are likely to be the same. It is important therefore to gather as much information as you can at the earliest possible opportunity. This is easy to do and has two benefits:

- You will demonstrate to the interviewer your interest in the job
- You will feel more confident knowing that you are well prepared

We suggest that you research three areas:

- The interview
- The job
- The organisation

By researching, you lessen the risk of feeling that you could have made a better impression or that you haven't done yourself justice. In addition, you place yourself ahead of the competition.

The interview

If you have been invited for interview, you need to know some basic facts, and if this information isn't supplied, you need to start your investigations.

> *Investigating the interview*
> * How to get there
> * Who will interview you
> * The format of the interview

How to get there
Finding out how you get to the interview is essential before you start your journey. Once you know the location, you can decide how you will travel. Always aim to arrive early – calculate the journey time and add an hour. Whatever method of transport you choose, delays may happen which are often out of your control. Also check what security arrangements there are, as they may add time to your journey.

On larger sites, leave yourself plenty of time to get from the reception to the interview building. Some people prefer to go on a practice journey as it gives them the opportunity to view the site at close quarters without the interview looming.

On the day   If you are delayed, be sure to contact the interviewers and let them know why you will be late and when you expect to arrive. Make sure you have the relevant phone number handy. They will appreciate your call as they may need to make other plans or reschedule.

On arrival   Having arrived early you will have the opportunity to make last minute preparations:

- Think through your replies and questions
- Get a feel for the organisation
- Complete any further application forms
- Read through literature
- Take advantage of other information
  - video
  - trips around the site
- Read your cv again
- **Relax**

Who will interview you
The key information you need here is: name(s), position in the organisation and job title.

There may be a number of interviews, particularly for a senior post. The first, in-depth interview, is often held on a one-to-one basis with a recruitment consultant, line manager or member of the human resources department. It could take the form of a thorough exploration of your CV or a structured interview.

Candidates short-listed from the first interview can expect second and third interviews, which are likely to be conducted by one or more senior staff, who may have responsibility for the post or an interest in it. The objectives for these interviews are to explore any aspects still outstanding from the first interview and to assess how well your personality will blend with the team. You may meet the same interviewer more than once – so learn to pace yourself and aim to remember names.

Knowing who is going to interview you will help you prepare responses. Interviewers' interests may fit into the following categories:

Organisational role	What they are looking for
Functional head	qualifications/experience ability to perform tasks understanding the job/technical jargon transferable skills match with management style expectations and culture
Managing director	ability to meet targets contribution to growth and profitability adaptability aspirations

Peers	team working
	personality
	style
	shared experiences
	experience
Junior staff	management style
	openness
	approachability
Human resources	your background
	career patterns
	training/development needs
	salary
	benefits
	start date

Some organisations employ recruitment consultants to short-list candidates and ensure that only the most qualified go forward. They will be seeking the person who most closely matches the employer's specification, not solely in terms of experience, but also in personality and aspirations.

The format of the interview

Interviews can take many forms. The two most common are one-to-one and panel interviews. Some organisations combine different types by short-listing candidates with a telephone interview, inviting them to a panel and then asking them to return for further one-to-one interviews. Once you have found out the format, you can gear your preparation specifically to suit.

Interview formats
- Telephone
- One-to-one
- Panel
- Tests
- Presentation
- Socials

Telephone   The informal pre-interview chat is often over the telephone. This may occur when the interviewer is uncertain whether to short-list you. For you, this call could be very important, making the difference between winning a face-to-face meeting or not. Anticipate this by keeping a checklist by the phone.

One-to-one   This is the most common type of interview, and consists simply of one interviewer talking to one applicant. It is the easiest interview to arrange and conduct and, in consequence, is the type most commonly used.

However, decisions are rarely the result of one person's perceptions. It is common to hold a series of one-to-one interviews, which may be on the same day, or could extend over months.

Panel   The panel (or 'selection board') may number from two members upwards. It can take many different forms, from a free for all, where all interviewers chip in with a variety of questions, to a more formal and structured approach where interviewers will take it in turn to ask questions reflecting their particular interests. At first, this style of interview may feel more threatening, but tends to be fairer and more equitable.

Panel interviews can be very formal. Responses and further exploratory questions are not always forthcoming because of the limitations of time. It is also more difficult to establish the same feeling of rapport as you can in a one-to-one interview.

The chair of the panel is usually the one who makes the initial introductions and the final remarks. Do not assume that they have the greatest influence in making final decisions. It is often difficult to know who to talk to –

- Always look at the person questioning you
- Direct your answer to the questioner
- Glance around to show you are ready for the next question

Do not be unnerved by the panel; treat it as if it is a one-to-one interview concentrating your attention on the questioner at all times. Only include the other members when you are ready to continue with the next question. Do not be put off by signals between members of the panel.

These probably have little to do with you personally but are more to do with matters such as time and questions.

Tests   Tests are now commonly used to help assess candidates' abilities, aptitudes and personality. They are not an examination of your ability to remember facts but an extra way of gathering information. All applicants will be given the same questions, tasks and parameters. In an assessment centre format these are carried out in groups.

Test type	Measures
Aptitude	Specific skills for the job: verbal, numerical, spatial, mechanical, clerical
Psychometric	Personality traits and preferences which may be needed to fit into team/project, temperament, disposition
Attainment	Knowledge of procedures, skills: driving, typing, technical terminology
Intelligence	General intellectual potential, problem-solving skills
Physical	Health, eyesight, colour perception, hearing acuity
Group discussions	Communication, judgement, reasoning, problem-solving, persuasiveness, listening skills, respect
Presentations	Ability to stand up and speak, arranging information, quick thinking, flexibility
Written exercises	Clarity, legibility, summarising

If you know there will be some form of test, remember to answer it honestly. If you attempt to paint a picture of yourself as the type of person you think they want, you will have to keep up the pretence or fail later on. Also many of the tests are sophisticated enough to detect deception.

Presentations   It is increasingly common for interviews to include a formal presentation as part of the process. You may get advanced warning of this and the particular subject area you are required to present. Be sure to check what equipment will be available to you on the day, overhead projector, slide projector, laptop, software, flipchart, etc. and who will constitute your audience. You may want to make copies of your presentation or a summary to hand out.

Occasionally you receive the subject on arrival you receive the subject on arrival at the interview and have to prepare there and then. Think through an outline of a presentation – how and in what ways you would address the issues of the day. Then all that you need to do if you are faced with this scenario is to adapt it to the specific requirements of the topic.

Presentation content
- Convince them that you are qualified and experienced
- Demonstrate successes
- Outline your contributions on a strategic and detailed level
- Establish good relationships

Be sure to inject
- Professionalism
- Degree of formality
- Controlled enthusiasm
- Pace and drive

A presentation is an ideal opportunity for you, but only if you can control your nerves and are clear about the messages you want to communicate. It is likely that this presentation will be in some way related to the job in question and most particularly to the main area of responsibility. Presentations can also be used to establish a relationship with the interviewer.

You should also consider whether it is appropriate to take a portfolio with you containing samples of your work. To be helpful, such things must be clearly relevant and be easy to handle and look at during an interview.

Socials   Part of your interview day could include meeting the team or a tour of the organisation. Some organisations arrange social gatherings where you, the other candidates and sometimes partners meet together with your future employers. These may be labelled informal events, but never be off your guard; they are a part of the interview process. Use this as another opportunity to gather information. Be sure to talk to all those representing the organisation and limit your consumption of alcohol.

The job

The essential starting point for success is to know as much as you can about the job for which you have applied. There are several potential sources of information; you should use as many as possible. These include:

- Preliminary discussions
- Personal contacts – your network

Preliminary discussions
You will have received some information about the job which attracted you enough to make the initial contact. You may want to know more about:

- Extent of duties and responsibilities
- Desirable and essential qualities required
- Skill levels, academic qualifications
- Reporting relationships
- Opportunities for training and development
- Location
- Hours of work
- Salary and benefits

Personal contacts
You may decide to collect information about the job by talking to someone involved in the recruitment process. If

you remain unsure about any particular aspects of the job or the organisation, you can save everyone's time by research. This is your opportunity to check fit and suitability – yours and theirs.

- Does your network extend into the organisation?
- Who do you know who works, or has worked, for them?

By talking to insiders you can get an 'inside' view. Remember that you will be hearing a subjective perception. Their views may be affected by personal circumstances or prejudices. So concentrate on facts rather than opinions.

The organisation

The interviewer will expect you to have some knowledge of the organisation. It is unlikely that it will be either comprehensive or complete. You need to show your interest not only in what you know but in filling in the gaps.

If sufficient information is not already supplied you should try to find out:

- What the organisation does
- Product details
- Ownership (public, private, group, independent, UK)
- Size
- History
- Structure (site, area or department)
- Management style
- Culture
- Staff turnover
- Outlets/factories/offices
- Present degree of prosperity
- Market position
- Stability
- Reputation
- Strengths
- Weaknesses
- Markets
- Competitors

The organisation itself and, if it is large enough, its public relations or customer services departments, are excellent starting points.

Other potential sources of information, their website and directories.

Directories

Key British Industries (Dun and Bradstreet) – basic corporate data on Britain's top 50 000 companies. Includes full contact details, names and titles of executives, financial details and industry

Kompass (Reed Information Services) produces *Regional, Product and Service Directories* on over 40 000 leading companies. Includes contact names of directors, executives and department heads, nature of business, annual turnover

Who Owns Whom (Dun and Bradstreet) includes parent companies, subsidiaries and associates

Directory of Directors – lists 60 000 directors of British companies and their directorships

On-line Databases

Reuters Textline – holds up-to-date articles on companies from the UK and international press

Kompass, *Key British Industries* and *Who Owns Whom* are also available on-line *www.kompass.net*

www.dnb.com – free business directory, searching by business name or product/service

These directories and databases are available from good public and business libraries. More detailed information is available from Companies House.

Companies House
Crown Way
Cardiff, CF14 3UZ
Tel: 0870 3333636
companies–house.gov.uk

The Internet

The Internet is also a good source of information and many organisations now have their own home page. For further information try *The Financial Times* home page – www.ft.com.

Use your networks, arrange to talk to your contacts and if possible, borrow literature not normally given out to the public. Recruitment consultants are another good source of information; they should be able to help you access the formal information in the form of annual reports, sales literature and house magazines. They can also provide you with an insight into informal information: personalities, problems and opportunities. Use everything that is to hand.

It is more than likely that you will use the telephone for some or all of your enquiries. Be sure to have thought through and have listed in front of you the questions you propose to ask.

- Job for which you are being interviewed
- Who will interview you – name and job title
- Format of interview
- How long you will be there
- Name, address and telephone number of the organisation
- Name, address and telephone number of interview location
- Date, day and time of the interview
- Availability of car parking facilities
- Security arrangements
- Name and title of person who is arranging the interview
- Job location
- Annual reports

You may also want to ask about salary and benefits. It can save you time if you decide at this stage that you are no longer interested as the salary is too low. Although there is also a cautionary note as salaries are often negotiable within parameters, but the person on the telephone may not be aware of these parameters and the level of flexibility.

These days you may be greeted by a message rather than a person. Consider and write down what you want to say before making the call. The key information you need to leave is:

- Your name
- Your contact telephone number, and
- Your address

- A brief message, requesting information
- Your deadline if you have one
- Your availability
- Repeat your name and phone number

Summary

Today we have guided you through the research you need
to do to prepare yourself for success. No preparation will be
wasted, so invest time and energy into gathering as much
information as you can at this stage. Have you:

- Researched the interview?
  - how to get there
  - who will interview you
  - the format of the interview
- Researched the job?
  - asked the questions
  - used your contacts
- Researched the organisation?
  - investigated directories
  - read Annual Report

Completing this research serves two purposes. It helps you
prepare yourself for the interview so that you present
yourself in the best possible light. It also helps you become
clearer about your suitability.

Know yourself

Self-knowledge is an essential ingredient of your preparation for the interview.

We have already suggested that you research the interview process, the job and the organisation so that you are better informed about the process and will know what to expect. A most important ingredient in this preparation is finding out about **yourself**, so you feel comfortable in presenting yourself to the interviewer.

This idea may seem a little strange: after all, if you don't know yourself, who does?

Today we will help you to know yourself better through a process of reflection. We will give you areas to think about and guidance. Complete all the exercises and be brave, and test them out on colleagues, friends, in fact, on anyone you trust.

You the person

When managers are asked to describe themselves, they tend to talk about what they do rather than who they are. They think of themselves in terms of their title and describe themselves as such. Operations Manager, Personnel Manager, Finance Manager or Project Manager are on many occasions sufficient descriptions and speak for themselves. Do not expect that this will be enough at an interview. You need to understand and describe what skills make up your role and what makes you successful and different.

Being invited to attend an interview suggests you match the interviewer's specification; you are halfway to success. However, it is unlikely that you will be the only person who looks good on paper. The interview is your opportunity to stand out and be noticed. You want to convince the interviewer that you can bring enhanced benefits to their organisation as well as being able to do the job.

To be successful, you need to make a firm impression and be different. The interviewer may see many interviewees in the course of a day, so the ones they will remember are the ones who are distinctive, who have something interesting to say

or who can make a unique contribution to the organisation
or department.

The key to presenting yourself is to consider and
understand your uniqueness. Ask yourself the following
questions:

> • What have I got that makes me special?
> • What makes me fit?

The answers may come easily or you may have to return to
these questions at the end of today when you have a clearer
understanding of you. The first step in building up a picture
of yourself is to appraise your skills.

Your skills

> • What can you offer us?
> • What are your skills?

These common interview questions, whilst apparently
simple, require thought, preparation and a level of
introspection and reflection. Your answer should not simply
be a regurgitation of your cv, relating what you have done.
It is more about when and in what contexts you have
performed well and the skills and competencies, contacts
and knowledge you have applied or acquired in the process.

Try to answer this question honestly and spontaneously:

> • What can I do?

How comfortable would you feel about presenting these
ideas to an interviewer?

It can feel strange at first to 'blow your own trumpet', but in an interview you are the only one who knows the tune.

The following list of national standards are contained in the MCI Occupational Standards for Management, they are basically a set of 'can do' statements. Look down the following list and mark whether you are:

1   Very competent

2   Competent

3   Adequate for the task

4   Undeveloped skills

Check afterwards with a colleague and see if they agree with your assessment. You may find you have been overly critical.

Maintain and improve service and product operations
- Maintain operations to meet quality standards   1 2 3 4
- Create and maintain the necessary conditions
  for productive work   1 2 3 4

Contribute to the implementation of change in services, products and systems
- Contribute to the evaluations of proposed
  changes to services, products and systems   1 2 3 4
- Implement and evaluate changes to services,
  products and systems   1 2 3 4

Recommend, monitor and control the use of resources
- Make recommendations for expenditure   1 2 3 4
- Monitor and control the use of resources   1 2 3 4

Contribute to the recruitment and selection of personnel
- Define future personnel requirements   1 2 3 4
- Contribute to the assessment and selection of
  candidates against team and organisational
  requirements   1 2 3 4

Develop teams, individuals and self to enhance performance
- Develop and improve teams through planning
  and activities   1 2 3 4
- Identify, review and improve development
  activities for individuals   1 2 3 4
- Develop oneself within the job role   1 2 3 4

Plan, allocate and evaluate work carried out by teams, individuals and self
- Set and update work objectives for teams and
  individuals   1 2 3 4
- Plan activities and determine work methods to
  achieve objectives   1 2 3 4

- Allocate work and evaluate teams, individuals
  and self against objectives   1 2 3 4
- Provide feedback to teams and individuals   1 2 3 4
  on their performance

Create, maintain and enhance effective working relationships
- Establish and maintain the trust and support of
  one's subordinates   1 2 3 4
- Establish and maintain the trust and support of
  one's immediate manager   1 2 3 4
- Establish and maintain relationships with
  colleagues   1 2 3 4
- Identify and minimise interpersonal conflict   1 2 3 4
- Implement disciplinary and grievance
  procedures   1 2 3 4
- Counsel staff   1 2 3 4

Seek, evaluate and organise information for action
- Obtain and evaluate information to aid
  decision-making   1 2 3 4
- Record and store information   1 2 3 4

Exchange information to solve problems and make decisions
- Lead meetings and group discussions to
  solve problems and make decisions   1 2 3 4
- Contribute to discussions to solved problems
  and make decisions   1 2 3 4
- Advise and inform others   1 2 3 4

Reproduced by kind permission of MCI

The above checklist may help to define your skills and give you the language to talk about them. The next step is to own them. People are generally poor at recognising their own skills, whilst often being good at identifying skills in others. If you are struggling with this, ask for feedback from the people you manage, or those who manage you; alternatively, think back over past appraisals and feedback you have received. Take some time to tell yourself about your skills, hear yourself saying them out loud without feeling embarrassed or apologetic. Practise in front of the mirror.

Your limitations

You are very likely to be asked about your weaknesses at the interview. We would prefer to think of them as limitations or areas for improvement and look for positive ways of presenting them. For example, you know that you can be impatient, but looked at from an alternative perspective it could be seen as an over eagerness to get things done. This is not hiding from the truth it is putting an affirmative interpretation on negative characteristics.

Your 'weaknesses' can also be listed to give you an idea of what changes you might want to make.

- What limits me?
- What has held me back in my career?
- Under what circumstances have I felt most frustrated and unhappy at work?

Your strengths

Skills are only part of the picture. They will help to show
what you do. You have individual strengths which will
dictate **how** you do things. This is what makes you unique.

The following list outlines the strengths of successful
managers. Look at it and see where their talents coincide
with yours.

Mark yourself on a scale of 1 – 4: 1 = always, 2 = frequently,
3 = sometimes, 4 = never

1 2 3 4

- Quick thinking and getting to the point
- Enthusiasm
- Presence
- Ability to handle conflict and make decisions
- Self-confidence
- Strength of will
- Commitment and determination
- Flexibility and willingness to change
- Creativity
- Willingness to take responsibility
- Initiative
- Competitiveness
- Sensitivity to people and situation
- Stamina
- Commercial awareness
- Judgement
- Being personally organised
- Ability to take risks
- Ability to strike the balance between
  big picture and detail

Using the list above for guidance, try to answer the following questions about your strengths. Be as specific as possible and add descriptions of how you utilise them.

- What are the strong points of my character and personality?
- In so far as I have succeeded, what has helped me?

Understand your achievements

The most practical way to assess yourself is to make a list of all your achievements, not solely the major ones, but everything that other people should know about. People find this process difficult, so to help you we've given you some ideas. Add any more of your own.

Achievements might include:
• A new idea
• Reducing waste
• Turning around a bad situation
• Avoiding potential problems
• Improving customer relationships
• Results which improved
• Costs you managed to cut
• An activity simplified or improved
• A crisis averted
• Something you made
• A new skill mastered
• A group you led
• A problem solved
• Anything that had a happy ending

The essence of you

You have considered and listed your vast array of skills, strengths and achievements and examined your limitations. Now is the time to put them together to form a composite representation of yourself.

Write down a number of sentences beginning with the words 'I am', e.g. 'I am a manager'. Try to think of at least 15 of these.

Be specific
Expand these sentences to show yourself off. Add to the sentences by explaining and giving clear examples. Where

possible, angle the examples to match the post for which you will be interviewed.

Produce statements such as:

I am a good manager because I am able to motivate and develop people. In my last job I inherited a team who were bored with the weekly meetings and often strolled in late. I talked to them individually, found out their dissatisfactions and instigated a system of agenda setting that involved them all. As a result the meetings became fun and much more productive.

This is very different from saying: *I am a good manager because I have a MBA or I am a good manager because I have worked for 'x' for 20 years.*

You can see from this example that the way you describe yourself and the kind of language you use detracts from or adds to the image you portray.

As well as giving concrete illustrations, you also need to think about your language. Be confident and assertive using phrases like the following to illustrate your point positively:

- . . . which resulted in
- . . . so that
- . . . the benefit was
- . . . the advantage was

Dismiss all your tentative language such as:

- . . . I probably could
- . . . I think I can
- . . . I have been told
- . . . some people think I'm. . .

Summary statement

You may like to reinforce your other statements by developing a summary career statement about yourself. This has the advantage of creating the right impression in the mind of the interviewer. Produce a powerful statement about the type of person you are and the contribution you can make to the organisation. You are then able to create value in the eyes of potential employers and increase the idea of the benefits you bring.

Statements such as:

- I am a successful sales manager with a proven track record of building teams and winning high profile orders . . .
- I am a determined professional with experience across a wide range of technical products . . .

This statement should be brief and powerful, highlighting all the benefits in employing you. Be sure to practise saying this statement; often statements that look good on paper do not translate to the spoken word naturally. After hearing it you may need to adapt it. Also be sure that you feel comfortable with the statement; if there is any hint of uneasiness this will show.

Try it out before the interview and validate your perceptions against another reliable source. Use a friend or work colleague who knows you well. Looking at yourself through different people's eyes can demonstrate the different facets of you. Begin by trying to share your findings with a trusted friend or colleague. Ask them what skills they think you have. Ask them what areas for development they see in you. Ask them to comment on your transferable skills.

Self-esteem

Self-esteem is essential to everyone's well being and it is something that can grow or diminish depending on what is happening in our lives.

It can be divided into two parts:

Internal self-esteem Comes from your beliefs about yourself, accepting your strengths and limitations rather than striving to be perfect. You see yourself as equal to but different from other people rather than superior or inferior.

External self-esteem Comes from interactions with others. You respond to their reactions, opinions, and how they relate to you. You let them tell you how good you are.

Many people have an over-developed need for external, reflected self-esteem because their internal self-esteem is fragile. As you increase your internal self-esteem, you will lose some of your dependence on external self-esteem.

You may find you spend time rating yourself as better in some areas and worse in others. Internal self-esteem is not dependent on comparisons. It is your own assessment of your self worth. What you have developed today is a collection of ideas that reflect your strengths and achievements.

Summary

Modesty or traditional conditioning may have made today a challenging day.

- You the person
  - what makes you special
  - what makes you fit
- Your
  - skills – what you can offer
  - strengths
  - achievements
  - limitations
- The essence of you

It may help to think of the interview and approach it as if you were preparing for a product launch. At the interview, you are the product, your challenge is to convince the other parties to invest in you. To make that decision they need to know why and what the benefits to them will be.

Preparing yourself for success

Some candidates see interviews as threatening situations. They worry about what limits them, about how nervous they get, about what the interviewers will think of them, and about failing to do the job if they were appointed.

For these people, what stands in the way of conveying self-respect is their overriding fear of failing themselves and their expectations. Their fear of failure overcomes their need for achievement. To some, this fear can have a paralysing effect and can completely ruin the interview.

If this is a description of you then you need to begin thinking of yourself and your approach to interviews in a more positive light.

Prepare to succeed by:
- Thinking positively
- Making a good impression
- Looking prepared

Thinking positively

World-class athletes, amongst others, will confirm the importance of mental attitude to achieving the best performance. To give yourself the best possible chance at interview you will need to think yourself into a fully positive frame of mind. How you set about this will be a personal matter. But concentration on your strengths, and the certainty that you have the internal resources to cope with any difficulties will go a long way.

Some people find it helpful to relax quietly and picture their success, both at the interview and in the subsequent post. They imagine this in great and vivid detail, visualising the thoughts and sensations this will bring. Others treat themselves to something new, ensuring that they feel good inside and out.

However you go about this, it is in many ways the most crucial phase of the whole process of preparation. You need an inner conviction that you are important to yourself. If you do not feel a sense of your own well-being and self-worth, how can you convince others that you will be an asset to their organisation?

You have to think positively before you can act positively: 'Whether you think you can or you can't, you're probably right.' Henry Ford

---

Compare:
- Thoughts — 'I'm sure they just asked me to make up the numbers. The others are bound to be better'
- Feelings — hopeless, inadequate, apprehensive
- Outcome — poor impression, no conviction, unsuccessful interview

With:

- Thoughts — 'They've picked me from all the applicants. I must stand a very good chance'
- Feelings — calm, confident, positive anticipation
- Outcome — assured impression, mutual fact finding, beneficial interview

Aim to direct your energy away from worrying about the interview and towards effectively preparing for it. Consider it as an opportunity where you are both interviewing each other, not as a one-sided test. Most importantly, remember that of all the people who applied, they have chosen you to interview.

If you are not nervous about attending interviews, then you should have little problem in this respect. Try to monitor whether you may be seen as overconfident and not taking things as seriously as you should. This is a common mistake made by interviewers who confuse confidence with arrogance.

To be just a little anxious, a little apprehensive is good; it is generally facilitative rather than inhibitive. Only when you become very anxious do you begin to harm your prospects.

Making a good impression

People make up their minds about us in minutes. Never ignore this fact, particularly at an interview when you have a relatively limited time to make an impression.

Your initial impact is vital. You don't get a second chance to make a first impression.

First impressions

- Start well
- First moves
- Appearance
- Body language
- Your voice

Start well

Whenever two people meet for the first time, they automatically start by evaluating each other on the basis of the non-verbal cues they receive. You and your interviewer will be doing just that as soon as you meet, whether in the interview room or on the walk from reception. It is a subconscious 'weighing up' time.

The interviewer will often base their judgement on this initial impression and spend the remainder of the interview looking to reinforce their view. You may be judged by nothing more than how you walk across the room, the strength of your handshake, or when and how you sit.

Evidence is often sought to support initial impression. You should therefore do all you can to enter confidently, but not brashly, with a pleasant smile.

Do:
- Close the door behind you
- Walk forward confidently, body straight, head up
- Respond to offered handshakes firmly
- Wait until you are invited to sit
- Remain quiet but alert to the opening moves by the interviewer
- Allow them to take the initiative
- Be ready to respond appropriately

Don't:
- Shuffle in, head down with hands in pockets
- Carry a jumble of paper
- Crash into the room pushing out your extended hand
- Attempt to dominate an interview, especially in the opening stages

Appearance

It is essential that you dress the part. Your appearance reveals a great deal about your self-image, your values and your attitudes towards other people and situations. Differences in occupational status are associated with appearance, for example, the 'city' type, the 'power' dresser. More favourable qualities are often attributed to smartly dressed people. Those who are perceived to be attractive and well groomed are often treated better than those considered unattractive or inappropriately dressed.

For interviews, it is wise to find out the dominant style or accepted image of the culture you are trying to enter. If you can visit the organisation at lunchtime or the end of the day, go and see what people are wearing. If that is not possible, take a look at the organisation's literature which may contain photographs of employees and directors.

Beware of the danger of overdressing. A good benchmark is to decide how the holder of the job would be expected to dress, and go just one stage better.

If you buy a special interview outfit, accessories or shoes do ensure that they are comfortable. There can be nothing more distracting than shoes that pinch, a jacket too long in the arms, a material that creases or generally ill-fitting new clothes.

Also be conscious of colours. More sober colours are often recommended for interviews: blues, blacks, greys with contrasting shirts and blouses. Your choice of tie, blouse or scarf is also important; any extremes of colour or pattern will make an impact. Think about the messages your appearance conveys to others.

Pay attention to the finer points of turnout: finger nails, hair, shoes and jewellery. Avoid too much perfume or aftershave. They won't be noticed if they are acceptable – only if they are not.

Avoid drinking alcohol, smoking or eating highly spiced food just before an interview. Eat mints or use a breath freshener before; be cautious.

Body language
Non-verbally you can communicate far more than you may be aware of. Although you often concentrate on *what* you

are going to say – and it is important for self-confidence to do so – this must not be at the expense of *how* you say it.
Research shows that:

- Words account for   35 per cent of the message
- Tone of voice ⎫
- Body language ⎭   65 per cent of the message

Negative thoughts and tension trigger off anxious feelings. It is possible to block them off – think about the directives 'chin up', 'stiff upper lip' and 'swallow your feelings' – using our body to control them. Beware of different messages through your body that can leak out and undermine or contradict what you are saying. If you are thinking positively about yourself and the interview, then your body will give a positive impression too.

Focus your attention on the interviewer to the exclusion of everything else. Ensure that you are comfortable and relaxed in the chair provided. Whilst listening and giving the interviewer your full attention it is also important that you demonstrate this.

- Sit comfortably, in an upright but relaxed posture
- Rest your hands on the arms of the chair or comfortably in your lap
- Look at your interviewer with an interested expression
- Keep your head raised when you listen
- Nod intelligently whenever the interviewer tells you something
- Be relaxed

There are however things to avoid. The list below outlines some of the most common blunders that interviewees make. In some way, these all indicate a desire to escape, boredom or impatience either to speak or leave.

- Fidgeting, biting your nails
- Crossing arms or legs, clasping the chair or your upper arms
- Leaning backwards, looking away from the interviewer
- Gazing fixedly at some point in the room
- Becoming distracted by the carpet or a picture
- Pointing your body towards the door
- Kicking your foot or tapping
- Propping your head on the palm of your hand
- Yawning
- Staring blankly at the interviewer
- Scribbling on paper

Your voice

Your voice is crucial to the impression you make. Many people are self-conscious about their voices and accents and, fearing they will let them down, try to mask them. Often all this does is make them unintelligible. Your voice is unique and is part of what makes you who you are. So befriend it and rather than trying to hide your accent, concentrate on being heard and understood. If you use your voice skilfully, you sound confident, knowledgeable and enthusiastic

Always speak in a clear, steady voice. If you hesitate or stumble you will appear nervous and ill prepared. If you are concerned about your voice, take care not to attempt to hide it. You will appear tense and closed up. Speak in your natural voice. Don't try to change it to impress the interviewer. Avoid bad language, slang, or annoying phrases or words such as 'you know' and 'actually', 'with respect' and 'to be honest'. Inject confidence, happiness and enthusiasm into your voice.
A – v – o – i – d   m – o – n – o – t – o – n – e.

Listen to your voice and get used to it. Take one of your statements from yesterday and speak it into a tape recorder. Express it as if you feel proud and positive about it and you. Vary the words you emphasise and the way you say them. See how different you can make your voice sound.

Do:
- Pause and breathe deeply before speaking
- Speak slightly slower than normal
- Speak clearly, open your mouth
- Vary the tone to add interest

Don't:
- Rattle out words 16 to the dozen
- Mumble
- Cover your mouth as you speak
- Stiffen your jaw
- Talk to your shoes

Looking prepared

You may want to consider taking a folder with you. It is useful to hold your prompt notes, statements or questions. If not overused, this will give an air of efficiency. It can also help to reduce your nervousness and remind you of the two-way nature of the process.

Look and sound positive. Talk in a positive manner. If you're asked, 'Can you do this job?' – the answer must never be, 'I think so . . .' or, 'I hope so'. It should be, 'Yes . . . definitely'.

Be calm. Don't be distracted by interruptions. If the telephone rings or an interviewer's colleague enters the room, stay calm. Don't panic if you don't know the answer to a question. If you don't know, admit it. Also if your mind goes blank, don't worry. Take a deep breath and ask for clarification.

How you feel is essential to the impression you create. Use today as a practice.

Prepare yourself for success
- Remember your positives
- Start with a good firm handshake
- Close the door behind you when you've entered the room
- Walk and stand tall
- Maintain eye contact with the interviewer or each interviewer in turn
- Dress the part
- Speak well
- Indicate you are listening
- Try to maintain open postures
- Stay positive and calm
- Remember you are interviewing them too
- Relax

Summary

Having taken you through a process of preparation, you should now be feeling and thinking more positively and enthusiastically about yourself and your ability to perform in the job. One of the other important obstacles is to be able to respond to the questions asked in a manner which demonstrates this ability in a succinct and coherent fashion.

Responding skilfully

Your preparation for the interview is now well under way. Just like a student before an exam, you should be confident that you have completed your revision, and be eagerly awaiting the big day. Continuing with the imagery, it is now time to look back over past exam papers, examine the questions asked, and plan your answers.

As you would expect, an interview is full of questions. These tend to be the same for each applicant, providing the key points for comparison. We looked at types of questions on Sunday; today we will focus on their content and give you guidelines for responding.

It is possible to anticipate and prepare for many of the questions you will be asked in advance. Interview questions have common themes. These are likely to be:

- Self-assessment
- Work history and experience
- The organisation
- The job
- Management style
- Ambitions and motivation

One of the main objectives of the interviewer is to build an impression of the interviewee not solely based on experience and history. However, criteria/competency-based interviews will expect you to present evidence of your past experience and achievements.

Where interviewers are more interested in your
characteristics and how you see yourself, their questions are
likely to include:

- Reasons for applying for this job
- Creativity and problem-solving
- Adaptability
- Reliability
- Attitude to authority and colleagues
- Motivations and aspirations

Knowing yourself is essential. Completing the exercises and
answering the questions on Tuesday will have helped you
to formulate your answers.

Listed below are some of the questions frequently asked at
interviews. Think through your answers and read through
the guidelines on responding. It may help to jot your
thoughts down on paper. They can serve as a resource or
aide-mémoire for you for the future and something that you

64

can return to and improve on. You may want to record your answers on to tape and listen to them. Practise putting the right enthusiasm into them.

Consider how you portray yourself. You need to be sure that you can leave the interviewer with a positive impression. They need to be confident that you can do the job, fit with peers and contribute to the organisation as a whole.

Self-assessment

These questions aim to see how you sell yourself and how able you are to communicate that to others. They are usually very open questions that leave the direction of the answer up to you. Be sure your route is planned along the right road.

Tell me about yourself
Because this is often the opening question in an interview, be very careful that you don't talk too much. Keep your answer brief, covering topics such as early years, development, management style, significant events and people. Think about the type of job and organisation; what are they looking for? Choose the bits of you that best match. Be selective; for example, the early highlights and your technical skills may be less relevant to a management role than your proven management skills.

What are your weak points?
Weaknesses can be the other side of strengths. Having prepared yourself, you can make sure that limitations sound like strengths and again give examples. Always

admit to one (or if hard pressed a second) limitation; if you don't it suggests you don't know yourself very well.

> • I can take longer than others to finish a task, unless there is a deadline to meet. My weakness is linked to a strength – being very thorough

What are your strengths?
Focus these on the post applied for and give concrete examples. After reading Tuesday's chapter you will have plenty of successes to relate. Sort through them before you go to this interview and make them relevant.

> • I can quickly create a harmonious atmosphere with new clients. They feel relaxed and we can talk business straight away

What can you do for us that someone else can't?
Here you have every right to blow your own trumpet and sell yourself! Talk about your record of getting things done, give examples and be specific. Mention your skills and interests combined with your history of getting results.

This is your opportunity to illustrate your uniqueness and the benefits you can offer the organisation. You need to create an image of yourself as someone who stands out as a greater potential asset than any of the other applicants.

Work history

This section of questions focuses on what you can draw from your practical work experiences. It may be that there is little that differentiates you from the other applicants on paper, so the spotlight is on the way you present your employment and its relevance to date.

If you could start your career again, what would you do differently?
After a brief review of options, come back to something very like your work so far. You may want to add something different earlier in your career rather than starting again. It is fine to be content; explain why you are, rather than just saying you would change nothing.

* Now I realise how much I enjoy being a manager. I would have put myself forward for a management position sooner
* I knew when I was at school that I wanted to be a chief accountant. I planned my education and job applications to this end

Why are you leaving/did you leave your present position?
Beware of becoming defensive on this question. Prepare yourself well. If you are leaving your present position because of problems with people, problems in the market-place or because of withdrawn finances, you need to consider your responses carefully. Look to future opportunities rather than past problems. After all few decisions are the result of just one factor. They are usually due to a combination of circumstances.

Resist any temptation to criticise or blame other people for your problems. You need to be seen as taking some responsibility for what happens to you.

> • I believe everyone should manage their careers; I
>   now recognise the limited opportunities for me within
>   my current organisation and am actively seeking a
>   change

*In your current/last position, what features do/did you like the
most? Which the least?*
Be careful and positive. Try to enhance the picture of you
that the interviewer already has. Be sure to describe many
more features that you liked than disliked. When you
mention any you disliked, describe ways in which you
overcame them.

> • I believe in regular communications and I had to
>   work hard to win my colleagues over to a similar
>   belief; we now have systems that I am proud of

*What were your most significant contributions in your last
position?*
Have specific examples ready. Link these wherever possible
to the achievements you have on your cv and the post in
question. Ensure that these give a balanced impression of
you. You may want to describe the contributions you made
through managing and developing people, or to areas of
development.

Did you think of leaving your present position before? If so, what held you there?

What makes you stay in any particular job and what prompts you to start looking for other opportunities? It may be challenge, colleagues, culture, influence, etc. Ensure you communicate that you know what is important to you at work and that you take control when things don't appear to be going right.

Would you describe a few situations in which your work was criticised?

Be specific. Think about constructive criticism and times when you've asked for feedback. You may then want to relate this to changes you've made to the way you work.

- I once lost my temper with a particular member of staff. It helped me think about the way I give and receive feedback

How do you react to pressure and deal with deadlines?

Observe that both are facets of your career, give examples from your experience in which you triumphed. You may also want to highlight what you have learnt to help you deal with the pressure to ensure it doesn't exhibit itself as stress.

The organisation

The interviewer will want to know how well you match their organisation. You are both looking for a good fit; they want someone who will easily slot in and you want somewhere you will feel comfortable. All your research should prepare you well for these questions.

What do you know about our organisation?
This question often precedes the interviewer's relating of a brief summary on the organisation. Ideally, you should be able to discuss products or services, reputation, image, goals, problems, management style, people, history, philosophy. Your research from Monday will help you here. Let your response demonstrate that you have done the research, but don't overwhelm the listener. If you don't know much about the organisation it is better to say so than to flannel.

Why do you want to work for us?
Relate this to the organisation's needs. Your research may have shown that the organisation is doing things you would like to be involved with. For example if the organisation is well known for a particular style of management, your answer should mention wanting to be a part of that. You should clearly identify what your contribution would be.

How long would it take you to make a meaningful contribution to our organisation?
Be realistic. You may want to ask for further clarification on

what the interviewer means by a meaningful contribution, or suggest what the most meaningful contribution could be in the short, medium and long term.

How long would you stay with us?
Be honest. Whilst obviously interested in a career within their organisation you can outline what would encourage you to stay. This may be challenge, recognition, variety, etc. You may want to highlight your demonstrated loyalty and commitment to your employing organisations.

- I expect to be a senior manager within five years and would be happy to achieve that within this organisation

What important trends do you see in our industry?
Be prepared with two or three. You may consider technology, economic conditions, political climate, responding to market demands or increased global competition. Be sure that you are up to date with your information. Read the relevant journals or papers as part of your preparation.

The job

This is the second part of the matching process. If you fit
into the organisation, do you have the requisite skills and
personality to do the job?

*What do you find most attractive about this position? What seems
least attractive to you?*
List three or four attractive features and one single
unattractive one. Put a positive suggestion with the less
attractive attribute.

> • I would like to look closely at the budgetary control
>   system as there seems to be scope for
>   reorganisation

Why should we appoint you?
Be prepared for this as it is a common question. Be clear in
your statements of your uniqueness and the ways in which
you match their requirements regarding experience,
strengths and characteristics.

What do you look for in a job?
Keep your answer oriented to the opportunity in question.
You could focus on your desire to perform and be
recognised for your contributions or on your interest in
working within that particular organisational environment.

> • I look for autonomy which is clearly the way you
>   expect your managers to work

If you could do any job, what would it be?
Hopefully your ideal should be similar to the job you have
applied for. Describe what an ideal job looks like to you in
the context of the organisation and culture. It should be
evident from this why you have applied for the job. If not,
then compare these ideals to the job you are applying for.

Management style

What is your management style?
Through your research you should know a little about the
organisation's styles of management. Find out about general
management theory too. Be honest whilst demonstrating
how your style will help you work smoothly within the
organisation.

Are you a good manager? Can you give me some examples?
Keep your answer achievement and task oriented. Think
about examples that demonstrate your success as a manager
and the different aspects of this. Always talk of yourself in
the first person, 'I am' rather than 'I have been told'. The
latter can sound as though you don't believe it.

Do you consider yourself a leader?
This is a closed question, do not simply respond with a yes
or no answer. Describe examples of leadership from your
experience: leading a team, areas of responsibility, the
organisation.

What do you think is the most difficult thing about being a manager?
You could mention planning, implementation and budgets. Although what is often cited as the most difficult task is to motivate, manage others and change the culture.

In responding, there are also some areas to beware of.

Don't:
- Let the interview become an interrogation
- Use weak evasive phrases: 'I have been told'
- Lie
- Be a 'know it all'
- Make jokes, especially against the interviewers
- Speak ill of third parties
- Blame others for your shortcomings

Summary

Today we have given you real examples of questions and answers. Be sure to leave the interviewer with a positive impression of:

- You
- Your experience
- Your fit with the organisation
- Your interest in the job
- Your management style
- Your interests and hobbies

You must always think of the interviewers and of convincing them of your suitability. Have you answered the following questions when giving your answers?

- Can this person do the job?
- Will this person do the job?
- Will this person fit in?

Tomorrow we will focus on other skills which will help you through the interview, helping you keep control and end on a top note. We explore the questioning process in greater detail in the companion to this book – *Tackling Interview Questions in a week*.

Your moves

So far this week we have concentrated on the interviewee in a reactive role. Today, we will look at the interviewee from a different perspective. Identifying opportunities to be proactive, to ask your own questions or lead the discussion.

Your moves:
- Ask the right questions
- Keep on listening
- Effective expression
- End on a top note

Ask the right questions

You will usually be given the opportunity to ask your questions towards the end of the interview. This is your chance to fill any gaps in your knowledge about the job and the organisation and clarify the next step in the interview process. Even if they do not invite questions, you should make sure that you check whatever you need to know. Few things are worse than leaving an interview thinking, 'If only I had asked such-and-such!'

Good interviewers will offer plenty of chances for you to check your understanding about the post and the organisation throughout the interview. It is still a good idea to have questions prepared that are based on your initial research and preparation. These may change or evolve as the interview develops.

The questions you ask will depend on how much information you have already collected, and your particular interests in the job. They should reflect your eagerness to work for the organisation and show evidence of thorough research. The pattern we suggest relates back to the data you collected on Monday. Your questions may relate to:

- The job
- The organisation
- The interview process

Do not bombard the interviewer. Choose one or two critical questions only. Refer back to Sunday when thinking about the types of questions you ask. Remember you are still the interviewee so watch you do not reverse roles. The interviewer does not want to be interrogated.

Work within the time left for the interview. If appropriate, check with the interviewer about time and ask no more than can reasonably be answered within that time frame. You can always ask, 'who else should I be talking to?'

F R I D A Y

The job

Your questions about the job may fall into the following categories:

- Routine and difficult aspects of the work: day-to-day responsibilities, special projects
- Full responsibilities of the job: reporting lines (up/down/sideways), shared responsibilities
- Support and guidance available to you: flexibility of budget, mentoring, coaching opportunities, bonus schemes, welfare
- Amount of travel involved: relocation plans, other sites to visit
- How often your performance will be reviewed: company appraisal scheme, performance reviews, are these pay/promotion related?
- Training and development opportunities: in-house schemes, qualifications/competence-based training, conferences
- Promotion and career paths: company expectations, board appointments, directorships, senior appointments (internal/external)

Maintain the image you have portrayed throughout the interview. If you have focused on the fact that you are a team player, ask questions relating to the team. What are the interviewer's perceptions of its strengths and weaknesses? If you believe that you will be judged on your performance as a key factor, ask about performance indicators or the organisation's expectations over the next six months.

The following examples may help you formulate some
questions:

- Why has the job become vacant?
- What will you expect from me in the next six
  months?
- What are the key tasks and responsibilities?
- What is the biggest challenge facing this team at the
  moment?
- What are the strengths and limitations within the
  team?
- How do you review performance?
- What development opportunities are there?
- What would my future career prospects be?
- Is promotion generally from within?

The organisation
There may be some gaps in your knowledge about the
organisation. Keep your questions to areas that are not
sufficiently covered in the information you have previously
received during the interview.

Topics for questions about the organisation
- Structure of the organisation: hierarchical, flat,
  matrix, informal structure
- Success of the organisation: turnover, new products/
  services, UK/international markets, financial health
- Decision-making: briefings, consultations,
  communications
- Future strategy and long-term plans: mission,
  strategic plan, philosophy
- Staffing: contraction, expansion, outsourcing

These sorts of questions are essential to your decision-
making. Is this organisation really viable in terms of profits
and, if not, are funders, holding companies, bankers, etc.
prepared to continue backing it for as long as it takes?

People have made bad decisions about jobs based on
inaccurate information about the organisation rather than
based on their suitability and the attractiveness of the job.
Continue your investigations after the interview if you are
still interested. Research whatever sources are available;
contact suppliers, customers, professional bodies, etc.

The following examples of questions may help:

- Could you clarify for me the structure of the organisation?
- How has the market been developing for products/ services?
- How are decisions made?
- What problems do you envisage for the organisation?
- What plans are there for reorganisation, expansion or retrenchment?
- What are your strategies for growth?
- How often do you update your business plan?
- What is the annual staff/financial turnover?

The interview process
You need to know what will happen once you have left the interview room. The interviewer should already have told you at the start of the interview, or the information may have been part of the advert or your invitation to the interview. If you are still not sure, ask. It is your right to have clarity about the procedure. The following examples may help:

- When will I hear from you?
- What is the next step? Further interview, medical, psychometric tests, social gathering?
- How will I be informed? Letter, phone call, fax, email?
- Is there further information you need from me?
- Is there someone else I should see in the organisation? Name, title, responsibilities?

Your prepared questions will serve you well, be sure to
remember:

- Don't ask questions about information you have
  already been given
- Don't ask questions for the sake of it
- Do ask supplementary questions
- Demonstrate you have digested the information
  previously given

Keep on listening

Throughout the book we have implicitly referred to the
importance of listening to and understanding what the
interviewer is asking or saying to you. We believe it is
equally important to keep on listening when you are asking
the questions. As the interview progresses and your time to
ask questions approaches, be careful not to lose
concentration. Many of the worst mistakes at interviews
arise from candidates who fail to hear or understand the
questions or statements that are made to them. If you're not
sure what the interviewer means, ask for clarification; it
doesn't mean you're stupid! In fact just the opposite.

Too often, interviewees are in such a hurry to speak, usually
out of nervousness, sometimes out of overconfidence, that
they do not fully hear what has been said.

There is also the danger that you hear what you expect to
hear rather than what is actually being said. Avoid
preconceptions; let the interviewer answer your questions
fully rather than prejudge the outcome or response.

Aids to listening
- Give the other person your full attention, don't fidget
- Wait for them to finish what they are saying, don't interrupt
- Ask open questions for more information
- Regularly check your understanding; don't make assumptions
- Watch your body language
- Be open-minded, not prejudiced

Effective expression

You want to present yourself in the best possible light throughout the interview process. This will involve effective answering of the questions asked, but also grasping any other opportunities to make your case.

Do:
- Keep to the point
- Be clear
- Know the appropriate jargon
- Speak with confidence
- Keep your answers positive
- Be honest and open with replies
- Give plenty of concrete work-related examples
- Be enthusiastic
- Weigh them up

Keep to the point

It is essential that you keep your questions and answers brief. In a short interview, aim to take no longer than two minutes with each. Also be clear to answer only the questions you have been asked and ensure your answer is relevant.

Structure your statements to ensure that your message is clear. You can achieve this in a number of ways. To make the most impact, limit your reply to one subject at a time; the more you try to include in your answer, the less the interviewer will get from it. So take time to think about which subject is most relevant to the job, organisation or the interviewer.

Be clear

Clarity in reasoning and expression is a skill which can be developed. Your aim should be to present your responses in an interesting and intelligible way, so that the interviewers are not left confused or uncertain. Be specific and talk about examples; always ask for precise details.

Know the appropriate jargon

Be careful not to talk in technical, functional or organisational shorthand that may lose the interviewer. We tend to assume the same knowledge base as those to whom we talk. At an interview this can be dangerous.

But, be familiar with any jargon connected with the job or the industry so that the interviewer doesn't leave you behind.

Speak with confidence
Be confident in all that you present. If you are not confident it will show. Let your body language reinforce your words. Be natural, let them see and appreciate the real you.

Be enthusiastic
Enthusiasm is a wonderful quality; it is a combination of energy and determination. Enthusiastic people are those who enjoy what they are doing and convey this to their companions. They are free from self-consciousness and are more in control of themselves.

Weigh them up
An interview must, to succeed, be a two-way process. The interviewer will be trying (whether consciously or unconsciously) to find out how good the 'chemistry' or the rapport is likely to be. You should do the same from your side; few jobs are worth having if you are unable to get on with your boss. You should be alert for indications of honesty, efficiency, friendliness, and the other characteristics you want from your manager.

End on a top note

Do not assume the interview has ended until the interviewer makes it clear that it has.

Last impressions linger longer
There is a danger of relaxing too soon when the interview appears to be over and the interviewer is conducting you to the door. Fix in your mind the picture of yourself that you want the interviewer to keep and maintain, if you want to be sure that those last impressions are favourable. You should leave the interview room as you arrived, confidently but not brashly, shaking hands firmly and with a smile.

If you are still interested in the job, a short letter to the person you met is invaluable. You can thank them for the time they took to tell you about the job and the organisation. Remind them of the key benefit you would bring to the company and briefly restate your reasons for wanting to work there.

Summary

Be spontaneous but in control at the interview. It will help having completed the preparation. Remember to:

- Maintain eye contact
- Take your leave as smoothly and politely as possible
- Do not add any afterthoughts
- Try to resolve any outstanding issues
- Shake the interviewer's hand
- Thank them for giving you their time
- Follow-up letter with your key benefit

Putting it all together

We have come to the end of the week and your preparations are nearly complete. By this stage you should be feeling more confident about how best to present yourself in the interview. An interview is, after all, your chance to shine.

Throughout the week we have focused on areas such as, what to say, how to say it and what to do. Today, we will aim to bring it all together. When you first learn a skill or technique such as driving, word processing or chairing meetings, you are anything but natural. But with practice, these skills become natural extensions of you. Interviewing skills are no different.

Today we will focus on helping to remove *all* the blocks that prevent you from being yourself. After all your *unique selling point* is *you*.

Putting it all together
- Objectives
- Rehearsal
- Readiness
- Review
- Feedback

Objectives

As we discussed on Sunday, interviewers will have set their objectives before the interview and will have planned how these will be achieved. An interviewer's key objective is to find the right person for the job. Other objectives will reflect the stage of the interview; for example, in the final stages there will be greater emphasis on fit rather than skills.

As an interviewee, you should also set objectives. Your main objective is to be offered the job. However, there will be secondary objectives ranging from presenting yourself in a positive light, through to exploring the real culture of the organisation.

These objectives should help you become more concrete in preparing for the interview and clearer in the messages you should concentrate on *communicating*. This will help you make the impression that will bring attention to you as **the** candidate for the job rather than just another runner.

Rehearsal

No-one ever taught you how to be interviewed. If you are lucky, you may have attended a workshop on the subject or received some feedback on how you present yourself. It is more likely that the only experience you have had of interviews has been the real thing, for real jobs. You don't have the time to experiment; only poor performers get lots of interview practice. So you need to rehearse:

- Entrance
- Body language
- Voice
- Answers to questions
- The benefits you bring
- Asking your questions
- Taking feedback

Don't let the success of your future depend on trying to find out how you interview on the day. Take time to practise. Practice develops performance in most things; interviews are no exception.

Ask a colleague, your partner, anyone whose opinion you value or trust, to act as the interviewer then role-play the situation and take feedback. Before you participate in the 'interview' with them, show them your objectives, the job description and a prepared list of the kinds of questions you expect to be asked. Encourage them to ask their own questions too. Then you can see how you handle the unexpected.

Decide whether you wish to record this practice using either a video or tape recorder. You will learn more this way and much of it will be positive learning. The better the rehearsal, the better the performance.

Your entrance
Have the person in the role of interviewer meet you and invite you to sit down. Don't tell them the image you want to create; check their perception later. Even at rehearsal it is quite likely you will feel nervous. This is fine; you will feel less anxious on the day.

Your body language
We would encourage you to breathe deeply and relax in your own way. Sit upright in a comfortable position and look attentive. You are likely to be attentive if your body is. If you appear uneasy, the interviewer will pick that up through your body language and not hear your excellent responses. Here you can find out whether you have any nervous and distracting mannerisms to change.

Your voice
Can your 'interviewer' hear you clearly? Do you sound convincing and interesting? To which questions do you give most energetic answers? This can give you an idea of where your key interests lie. Listen to the rhythm in your voice; work at not being monotone.

Answers to questions
Experiment with the time you take to answer the questions.
Just how long are the silences between the questions and
your responses? Make sure to listen right to the end of the
question and make your reply clear and specific.

The benefits you bring
It is important to reassure the interviewer throughout the
interview that you are the person they seek. Introduce
examples and case-studies that reinforce your positive
statements. Remember to turn any weaknesses into
strengths and learning points.

Asking your questions
You will have some questions you prepared earlier; use the
rehearsal to practise asking unprepared questions too. How
clear and thoughtful are they? Be sure to keep them
specifically related to that job or company.

Feedback
After the rehearsal make sure you have plenty of time to
playback and discuss what happened. Listen carefully.

What can you improve? Also accept where you are strong
and feel confident about it. Keep practising if you can. Draw
up a checklist of the things you wish to rehearse and ask
your interviewer for comments and suggestions on it.

Readiness

Here are a few questions you might want to ask yourself just
before you go to the interview:

Am I ready?
- Are my clothes and shoes clean, neat and tidy?
- Is my hair tidy?
- Am I clear what image I want to project?
- Have I decided how to project that image?
- Can I be heard clearly?
- Am I walking/standing/sitting tall?
- Am I relaxed?
- Do I feel confident to answer the questions?
- Have I structured my answers for the best impact?
- Have I prepared a sheet of prompts/questions?

Review

By analysing and reviewing your performance after the
interview, you can see where you might need to improve
and so develop the necessary skills. This review should
take place as soon as possible after the interview. It will
help you to identify areas you need to strengthen if you are
attending any more interviews. One of the most important
questions to ask yourself is the one which began the week.

Answer this honestly: *Did I present myself in the best possible light?*

The following list will help you to review your interview performance systematically in more detail:

Did I:
- Arrive on time?
- Speak confidently to all employees you met?
- Handle the opening moments well?
- Feel and look relaxed?
- Maintain appropriate eye contact?
- Use the full range of your voice to convey your message?
- Stay cool and calm?
- Answer all the questions well?
- Expand your answers?
- Refer to your strengths?
- Listen carefully to the questions?
- Understand the questions before you replied?
- Work out in advance the points you wanted to make?
- Volunteer information when given the chance?
- Capture and hold the interviewer's attention?
- Impress the interviewer?
- Demonstrate your knowledge of the job and company?
- Ask good questions?
- Adapt and adjust your questions?
- Deal with the closing moments well?
- End on a confident, optimistic note?

These questions will give you an idea of what you need to improve. If your answer is 'no' to any of the questions, try to explore the reasons why and particularly how you could improve. Answer the following questions:

> - What impression did I create?
> - Which questions did I find it difficult to answer?
> - Did I say all I wanted to say?
> - What will I do differently?

The more you know about yourself, through this form of review and other forms of feedback, the better equipped you are to present yourself to others.

Interviews are so complex and artificial a process for all parties that no matter how thoroughly you prepare, some may not turn out as you hope or expect. Don't dwell on the interviews that don't go well, understand why and learn from them. Focus on success and success will come to you.

Feedback

You should also not be afraid to ask for comments from the interviewer. If they are not forthcoming request them. If there are areas that you suspect, or are told, consistently let you down, seek help or a second opinion. Investigate your local sources of help, such as:

- Colleges/adult education centres
- Business schools/universities
- Correspondence courses
- Learning and Skills Councils (LSCs)
- Guidance organisations
- Professional institutes: The Chartered Management Institute
- Videos and books
- Careers counsellors

Don't be afraid to ask. Educational establishments are responsive to their customers and if you have a need, approach them with it. If nothing currently exists then why not set something up, or organise an event through your local professional institute or with a group of colleagues. Practice is never wasted. Feedback and development are essential to your future success.

Above all enjoy the experience. The most valuable interviews are frank open discussions involving facts, ideas and opinions. By following a simple pattern you can achieve the success you want at interviews.

Simple steps to success:
- Do your research
- Know yourself
- Prepare yourself for success
- Respond skilfully
- Practise
- Review

As you are very well prepared, all you now need are our best wishes – good luck! We hope that you found the book useful. If there are any areas that are still unclear, then why not contact us at inform@inform-global.com. We would also appreciate your comments on your interview experiences.

*IN*FORM Training and Communication provides a professional, client-centred range of services. To discuss your needs in the areas of personal development, appraisal or environmental management please contact our office through the publishers